To all Intrepid Explorers -

The Explorer Files are designed to help you be in the know about this ancient castle, to prepare for your expedition, and then to be a souvenir.

Before you plan your trip we recommend checking Alnwick Castle web site for details of events. The falconry display, magic shows, etc, take place on certain days only. (www.alnwickcastle.com) Use the Explorer Files maps to work out your route round the Castle.

If you have time before you explore, fire up your imagination! It is so much more exciting if you have read some of the castle history beforehand. You will be able to imagine brave Hotspur and his knights setting out to protect towns and villages from Scottish attackers! Standing inside the castle walls, imagine the scene, in 1650, with Cromwell's soldiers guarding six thousand Scottish prisoners from the defeated Royalist army! Move forwards through time to the end of the eighteenth century and imagine the Percy Tenantry Volunteers training to fight, as they expect Napoleon's army to invade.

Alnwick Castle welcomes intrepid explorers of every age. Remember great adventures start here!

The KINGDOM of NORTHUMBRIA

Harry Hotspur

Real name, Sir Henry Percy, eldest son of the first earl of Northumberland. Born in 1364, killed in 1403, at the Battle of Shrewsbury.

One of England's most famous mediaeval knights, he was renowned for his courage and skill as a fighter. He was said to be good-looking too!

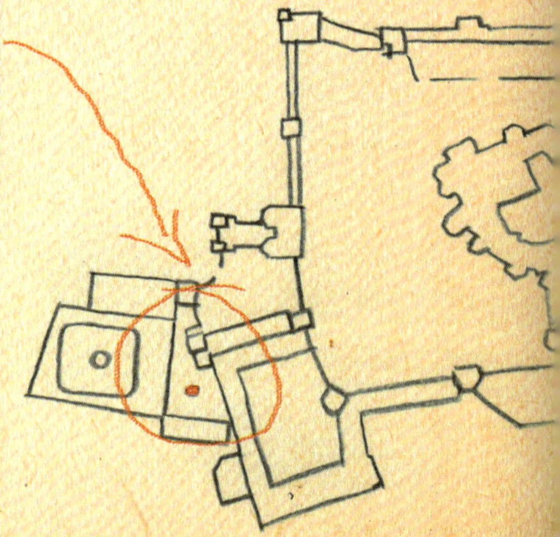

How Sir Henry came by his nickname, 'Hotspur'

What are spurs?

Spurs were used to make horses move faster. Spurs were attached to a rider's boots and they had sharp points. The rider would dig the spurs into the sides of the horse to urge it to move faster. There were two sorts: the rowel, which turned and looked like a star, with lots of sharp points, or the sort with one sharp point. Spurs were often presented to knights as prizes at tournaments.

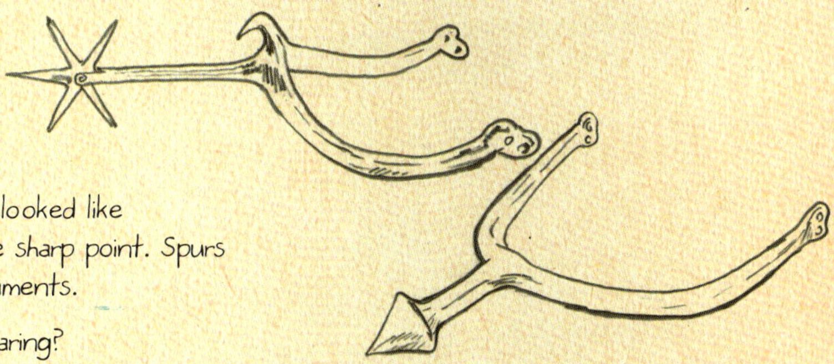

Have a look at the statue. Which type is Hotspur wearing?

Why 'Hotspur'?

Sir Henry gained his nickname, 'Harry Hotspur' at the siege of Berwick in 1378. The Scots had captured the fortress and killed its captain, Sir John Boynton. Then the earl of Northumberland and his forces arrived and besieged the castle. The siege lasted 9 days. The fifty Scottish defenders could see the young Sir Henry, aged 14, enthusiastically riding from one part of the siege to the next, helping his father in any way he could. The Scots noted his keenness, calling him 'Harry Hotspur'. His proud dad gave him the honour of leading the storming of the castle. He led the charge, brandishing his sword and shouting the Percy motto, 'Esperance!' – which means 'hoping'. There was not much hope for the Scots. Any Scottish survivors were killed. The siege was lifted and the captives freed.

Are there any other Hotspurs?

Other Hotspurs include several HMS Hotspurs, including one captained by Lord Josceline Percy during the Napoleonic War and an H class destroyer (launched in 1936), which was operational in World War Two.

There was also a Hotspur comic for boys. This started out as a story paper in 1933, and its last issue was published in 1981.

All of these Hotspurs are named after Alnwick Castle's own Harry Hotspur!

Hotspur? Anything to do with Tottenham Hotspur Football Club?

Yes! Tottenham Hotspur started in 1882 as the Hotspur Football Club. Some grammar school boys, who played for the Hotspur Cricket Club, founded the football club. They chose the name Hotspur because the Percy family owned land and a house nearby and, of course, because of Harry Hotspur's reputation as a great warrior knight.

Answer: Harry is wearing spurs with one sharp point

Hero or Hothead?

Hero

Years of Border warfare – usually raids and skirmishes – had built Hotspur's reputation as a brave and energetic soldier. He had also fought against the French and taken part in a crusade. He took part in one of the most famous tournaments of the fourteenth century at St Inglevert, in France. Hotspur jousted for Henry of Bolingbroke's team, to great acclaim.

King Richard II appointed Hotspur warden of the East March and keeper of Berwick. This meant Hotspur was responsible for protecting the eastern half of the border against Scottish raids.

Hothead?

Hotspur took part in three major battles as a general. His critics argue he was not a skilled general and more of a hothead.

The first battle, the Battle of Otterburn, took place in August 1388. In June of that year, the Scots had not renewed the peace agreement. The English realised that war was likely. They started to raise troops to defend the border. The new troops were men who were not professional soldiers. They were farm workers, shopkeepers and craftsmen, not trained fighters. Hotspur also had his own regular soldiers at his command.

In late July two Scottish armies invaded. One army was on the eastern side of the border. The main army was on the west. Hotspur and his force were in Newcastle.

The Scots, led by the earl of Douglas, rampaged south into County Durham, looting and causing chaos wherever they went. By the beginning of August they were heading back north and had made camp outside Newcastle. One account says that Hotspur and Douglas fought outside the castle walls and Hotspur was injured and lost the pennon (flag) from his lance. Douglas sent an insulting message to Hotspur. Hotspur's reply was to say that they would meet and fight before Douglas returned to Scotland.

Under cover of darkness, the Scots left Newcastle. Hotspur sent scouts after them. From their information Hotspur realised that this was not the main Scottish army.

Rather than wait for the Bishop of Durham with his troops, who were a day's march away, he and his men set off to catch up with the Scots. After a long day's march, Hotspur caught up with them at Otterburn, at sunset.

Those who think Hotspur was a hothead, say that he should have attacked the following day. He attacked before all his forces had reached Otterburn and as soon as he caught up with the Scots. His forces ended up being split – the left wing, commanded by Sir Matthew Redman, chased after some retreating Scots, while the right wing, under Hotspur, was defeated. The Scottish earl of March's forces attacked the weakest point of the English forces and broke through. Hotspur had to surrender. The earl of Douglas was killed in the fighting.

Hotspur had wanted to surprise the Scots. He did, but he did not get an advantage from it. It was a strategy that did not allow him to make good use of the English archers or to organise his troops.

The second battle was the Battle of Humbleton Hill, 14 September 1402.

In September 1402 the Scots invaded. This time they went as far as Newcastle.

The English forces gathered at Millfield. They would intercept the Scots on their way back to Scotland. Knights and men came from castle garrisons at Alnwick,

Warkworth, Dunstanborough, Harbottle, Roxburgh and Carlisle. This time the earl of March and his men were on the side of the English. The earl of Northumberland, Hotspur and the earl of March had carefully planned this trap, which cut off the Scots' retreat.

The Scots took up position on Humbleton Hill. The English decided how to attack. According to one witness, hothead Hotspur wanted to make an immediate charge against the Scots. The earl of March advised that the archers be used instead. The Scots were easy targets as there was not much cover for them. His advice was accepted. It was good advice. The tactics worked well and the Scots were defeated. Among the prisoners was the earl of Douglas.

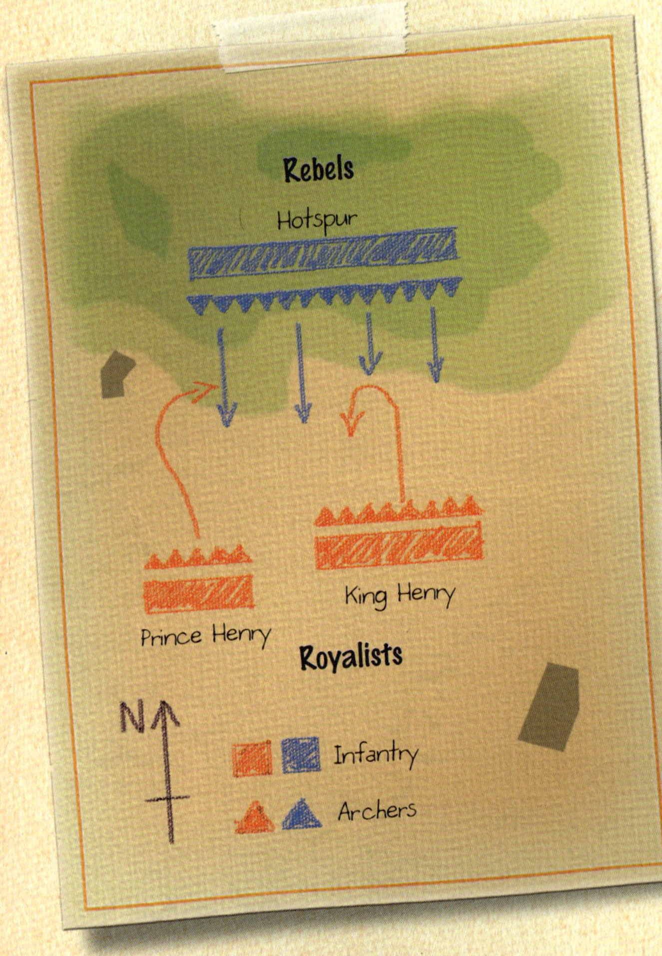

The third battle was the Battle of Shrewsbury, 21 July 1403.

The earl of March this time was on the side of Henry IV. Hotspur and his allies were rebelling against the king. At first things went well for Hotspur. His archers were effective against the king's infantry. The king then moved up his main troops. The rebels charged them twice but were pushed back. Hotspur and the earl of Douglas (now fighting for Hotspur) decided to lead a group of thirty knights and to fight their way through the enemy to kill the king. When they reached the royal standard (the king's flag showed where he was) they found two decoy knights dressed like the king.

They cut the knights down. The decoys had been more of the earl of March's clever tactics!

The battle continued. The rebels were outflanked by Prince Henry's troops and were now being attacked from the rear. Hotspur lifted his visor to survey the scene and was hit by an arrow. He died instantly. The rebels had been shouting 'Henry Percy King!' Now King Henry's army started cheering, 'Henry Percy dead!' Without their leader, the rebel army was defeated.

Was Sir Henry Percy a hero or a hothead? You decide!

He was certainly courageous and greatly admired, even by his enemies. Even King Henry wept when he saw the dead body of brave Hotspur. The King (previously known as Henry Bolingbroke) had been helped to the throne by the Percys. When young, Hotspur had been on a crusade with him and had been a member of his tournament team.

Hotspur's body was to be buried respectfully, not beheaded and cut up into quarters and displayed at city gates as a warning to other would-be rebels and traitors, as would normally be the case.

During his lifetime Hotspur had been a popular figure. All the young knights wanted to be like him, as Shakespeare says:

> '...and by his light
> Did all the chivalry of England move
> To do brave acts: he was, indeed, the glass
> Wherein the noble youth did dress themselves.'

Gruesome Grave Robbing!

Hotspur's body was taken from the battlefield by a relative, (Thomas Neville, Lord Furnival) and buried at Whitchurch.

However, there were rumours that Hotspur was still alive. The King had Hotspur's body dug up. It was put on show in the main street of Shrewsbury. After a few days it was salted, beheaded and cut up. The head was sent to York to be fastened above one of the gates and the quarters to be hung above the gates of London, Bristol, Chester and Newcastle.

In November, the parts of the body were returned to Elizabeth, Hotspur's wife. The re-assembled body was buried in York Minster.

Knights' Quest

Warrior strength, stamina and agility – learn the fitness secrets of the top mediaeval knights!

Warriors would build up their strength by training with swords two or three times heavier than they would normally use. They would practise sword cuts on a pell – a tall wooden post sunk into the ground.

Pages would start training by using wooden swords. Footwork is important in sword fighting. Knights, squires and pages would practise moves such as the 'backsteppe' (a back step with the rear leg) and the 'cock step' (a forward skipping step with the lead leg). They would practise different strokes such as the 'foyne' (a stabbing thrust with the sword) and the 'downright blow' (striking downwards with the forward edge of the sword). There was much to learn.

Knights were expected to be expert horsemen. Pages learnt to ride at an early age. They had to be able to control their horses with very little use of their hands. In battle, knights would be holding weapons such as lances, swords and maces.

Lance training started by being pulled along on a wheeled wooden 'horse' by fellow knights-in-training. You had to aim your lance at a shield nailed to a post suck into the ground. When you hit the shield, you needed to grip hard with your legs to stay on the 'horse'. You had to have a firm grip on the lance to keep hold of that too.

There was a school trip in Knights' Quest when we arrived – I don't know if the teacher enhoyed it as much as the kids!

Knight's Equipment

The statue gives us a good idea of the type of equipment Hotspur would have used.

The war horse

On the battlefield, Hotspur would ride a 'destrier'. This was a type of horse specially bred for its strong backbone. These war-horses were stallions. The horse had to carry the weight of a knight in armour. A good destrier would be very, very expensive. The horses would wear horse armour to protect them in battle. This would be made out of boiled leather (boiling makes leather tougher) and metal plates. The horse would also wear padding, to prevent the knight's armour rubbing.

The war-horses would look something like modern heavy hunter horses and would be powerful and difficult to control. The horses would be kept fresh for battle and led to the battlefield by squires. The knights would be able to mount the horses easily, despite their armour. Armour was designed to allow knights to move freely while fighting. Knights had to be able to mount and dismount quickly, as necessary.

How heavy was a knight's armour?

The knight's armour wasn't as heavy as you might think. The Royal Armouries say it would have weighed somewhere between 20.4–24.9 kilos (45–55 lbs). Hotspur would be wearing plate armour, as on the statue. There is some chain mail around the neck, which allows better movement.

The helmet on the statue does not have a visor. Knights in battle would wear them. The visors on the helmets did make it difficult to get a really good view, but were essential. The archers would be sending volleys of arrows into the battlefield and aiming in particular at the leaders. It is not certain how Hotspur was killed. One story is he had lifted his visor to survey the battlefield when he was hit in the face and killed by an arrow.

Hotspur is wearing coat armour. This is fabric armour lined with metal plates, whalebone or boiled leather (makes leather tougher). These were worn over a mail shirt or hauberk. Padded and quilted coat armour

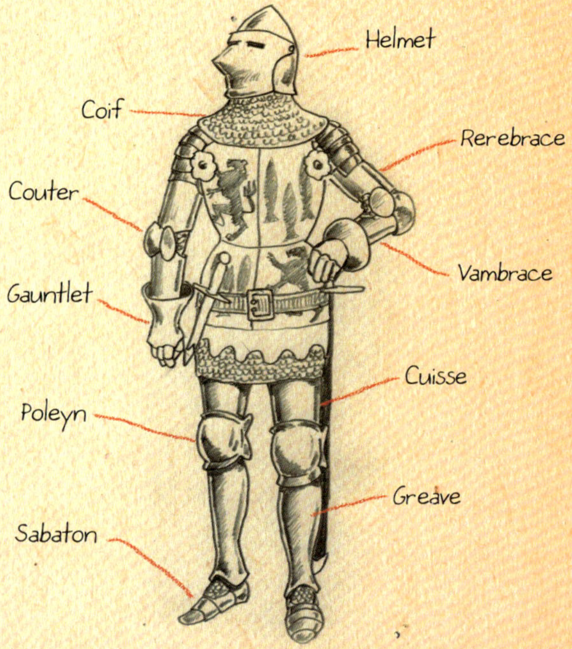

offered protection and could be decorated with the knight's coat of arms. What design is on Hotspur's?

Hotspur is also wearing plate armour on his arms, legs and feet and gauntlets to protect his hands. Notice his very trendy (for mediaeval times) pointed boots.

Weapons

Hotspur's sword was a long-sword. It would have a long straight double-edged blade. It had to be flexible, so it would have a flattened or hollow channel. It would cut through chain mail, flesh and bone. It was long enough for the mounted knight to attack foot soldiers. It could be used one handed or with two hands. The swords were short enough for knights to use whether they were on foot or on horseback. There were different types of sword: some were good for cutting, others for thrusting. Swords were developed to attack knights in plate armour and were more rigid and thicker than the earlier swords that had been used when knights wore chain mail armour.

Plate armour was nearly impossible to cut through with a sword. It had to be prised open, once it had been cracked and dented. Because of this, axes were popular (such as pole axes and halberds) and war hammers were also used.

Shields were not so important for knights wearing plate armour. The armour gave good protection.

Hotspur is holding a lance. In battle knights would charge with their lances, hoping to kill, injure or unseat enemy knights. Lances were also used in tournaments. Tournaments were sporting events that were good practice for war. One type of tournament was called the joust. Two knights on horseback, using lances, would try to knock each other off their horses.

Look at Hotspur's saddle. Notice how it is built up at the front and the back. Why would that be a good design if you were fighting another knight with a lance? Would it be easy to use a lance to push the knight off his horse?

Dragon Quest

In fairy stories and folk tales, the knight's traditional enemy was the dragon. Dragons were fierce and wily, some having a weakness for riddles! You will need all your wits about you to take on the challenge of the Dragon Quest!

Victorian Stables

The Knights' Quest area was not part of the original mediaeval castle. It was built as a riding school and stables in the nineteenth century.

Where were the stables in olden days?

When you go into the outer bailey, and are inside the curtain (defensive) walls of the old castle, think about where you would have put the stables. Not only would the horses sleep in the stables, but some of the garrison would too. The building would house the horses on the ground floor and the men would sleep in the hayloft on the floor above.

You would probably want to have the blacksmith's nearby (for fixing horseshoes), and the store for the horses' food (fodder).

Where would you put your hobelars (mounted soldiers)? If you thought that a good place would be near the barbican, the castle's fortified gateway, you were right. Not only would it be sensible from the point of view of having them near to the exit in case they had to ride to defend a town or village from Scottish attack, but also it was convenient for taking the horses out for exercise.

There were also more stables elsewhere in the castle, in the inner bailey.

Early history of Alnwick Castle

Motte and bailey castles

Alnwick Castle was built in Norman times. William the Conqueror's nobles built castles throughout England. The basic design they used was the motte and bailey castle. Their purpose was to keep the lord and his family safe and to make sure that the Normans kept control of the country.

The bailey was a wall around the castle, usually with a ditch on the outside. Generally, it was no more than an arrow's shot away from the keep (central castle building). This meant any attacker getting over the wall would be within range of the keep's bowmen. Alnwick Castle has a large six-acre site. This explains why so many towers were built and why there is an inner and outer bailey. The towers were good places for archers to shoot from and the wall that separated the inner and outer bailey provided additional defence.

The motte was a huge mound with a keep on the top. The sides were made steeper by a ditch dug at the bottom. It would be difficult to scramble up the sides. Attackers would also have to find a way of getting over the sharp stakes in the ditch.

Why were castles built?

Castles were built to provide safe places, which could be defended from attack by the soldiers who were based inside.

The castle is here because this is where the road to Scotland crosses over the River Aln. This is one of the routes Scottish invaders might have used.

It is a good site to defend because it is on high ground and attackers have to cross the Aln to reach the castle.

Bow Burn goes underground

Nowadays the Bow Burn is completely underground, but in earlier times it ran along the ditch by the eastern side of the castle, flushing away sewage from the guarderobes (toilets).

Entrances to Alnwick Castle

In Mediaeval times there were only two entrances. The first was the Gatehouse. The Barbican was added to strengthen it.

The second was the postern gate. The Postern Tower stands over it. At a distance, it is difficult to spot from the outside, unless you are familiar with the castle. The postern gate, or 'sally port', would be useful for the garrison. They could launch surprise counter-attacks on enemies besieging the castle, messengers could leave secretly and spies could sneak out to find out what was happening outside.

Building the castle

Yvo De Vesci began building the Alnwick Castle in 1096, and it was completed by his son-in-law, Eustace Fitz-John, who was made Baron of Alnwick. The castle has always covered the same area and parts of the early twelfth century masonry can still be seen here and there in the walls.

Eustace's son William took the name de Vesci, his mother's name, and the de Vesci family lived at the castle until 1297, when his descendant, also called William De Vesci, died.

This William had a young son, William Vesci of Kildare, and had arranged for Anthony Bek, the Bishop of Durham, to look after his son's inheritance until he came of age, but in 1309, Bek sold the castle and the barony of Alnwick to Henry Percy.

Was the castle bought in a dodgy deal?

There is a document that suggests that Anthony Bek was the owner of the castle and that the father had given Alnwick Castle and barony to Bek and had left his Yorkshire and Lincolnshire land to his son. However, the document had not been registered with the Exchequer.

William Vesci of Kildare died at the Battle of Bannockburn in 1314 and the first Lord Percy at Alnwick in 1315. After their deaths, rumours started that the sale of the castle was not legal.

Gilbert Aton, a relative of William Vesci, claimed that the castle was his. The second Lord Percy paid him a large sum of money and a marriage was arranged between his daughter, Isabel, and Gilbert Aton's son. In return, Gilbert Aton confirmed that the Alnwick Castle did belong to Lord Percy. Phew! So those rumours about Anthony Bek forging the document were untrue, after all!

The Barbican

The Barbican is a fortification built to defend the main entrance gate to the castle.

Anyone attacking Alnwick Castle here was in for some nasty surprises!

Rebel's son and rebel's grandson

What is really surprising about the barbican is that Henry built it at all. His dad, Hotspur, had been killed rebelling against the king. Two years later, his grandfather, the first earl of Northumberland, had also been killed rebelling against the king. The earl had sensibly left his grandson in Scotland, at the Scottish court, out of the reach of an angry King Henry IV. The English king seized the Percy castles, lands and possessions. The title, 'earl of Northumberland' was stopped. The King had plenty of reasons for not wanting to hear it ever again!

Harry Potter takes off!

If you look at area in front of the stretch of wall from the clock tower to the Barbican, it may seem oddly familiar. Have you seen the first Harry Potter film, Harry Potter and the Philosopher's Stone?

Yes? You may recognise it as the setting of Harry's first broomstick flying lesson!

Henry, Second Earl (or First Earl of Northumberland, version 2?)

Just how did the Percys recover their lands, possessions and the title?

After Henry IV died, negotiations started. In 1414 Henry Percy was 21 and old enough to claim his inheritance. After all, Henry had not been involved in any acts of treachery. The story also involves a marriage and a ransom. In October of that year, Henry Percy married Eleanor, the widow of Richard Dispenser. Eleanor's mother, Joan Beaufort, was the wife of the earl of Westmoreland and the aunt of the new king. Percy's mother-in-law is believed to have made it possible for Percy to have his inheritance restored to him. As part of the deal, Percy had to pay the ransom of the Duke of Albany's son. At the time the Duke of Albany was in control of the Scottish government. His son, Murdoch, earl of Fife, was an English captive. Percy paid the £70,000 ransom – a huge sum in those days. In effect, there was an exchange. Percy could return to England and Murdoch could return to Scotland

Percy's title, earl of Northumberland, was awarded in 1414. Technically, he was the first earl, not the second. To avoid confusion, he is referred to as the second earl.

How To Get Killed Storming the Barbican

The Barbican is a top-of-the-range fifteenth century fortification and was very high tech for the time. Hotspur's son, Henry, built it around 1464.

Did anybody manage to storm the Barbican? What do you think?

The Barbican was never taken by force. For some reason, enemy commanders preferred to use other ways of attacking the castle!

Drawbridge

The drawbridge is a see-saw design. The front part raises up to cover the doorway. The other half descends into the ditch.

The machinery to operate it is in an underground room where you can't get at it.

Somehow batter or burn through the drawbridge and then get to work on the portucullis.

Portcullis

The portcullis is a heavy, iron gate lowered by machinery in the room above, and held in grooves in the walls.

In full armour attempt to cross the deep ditch lined with wooden spikes. Break through drawbridge! Bring a very long battering ram!

Break down the iron portcullis. Then cross that deep ditch, avoiding those menacing wooden spikes. Clamber onto solid ground. Danger! More arrows fired through arrow loops! Bring battering ram!

Batter down oak gates! Danger! Earl's soldiers lying in wait! Drop battering ram!

Hand to hand combat!

The Abbot's Tower

This part of the castle has much of its original stone work intact. It dates from the time of the first Lord Percy (1309–15). The tower may have provided a refuge for the abbots of Alnwick Abbey in times of danger. The square watchtower has a good view of the direction trouble usually came from. The tower was an early warning station, as a fire lit at the top could be seen a long way away and would send a signal that enemy forces had been sighted. People would have time to get ready for an attack.

Hidden treasures in the Royal Northumberland Fusiliers' Museum

This museum houses many treasures, including items dating back through the centuries from the 17th century origins of the regiment to the Fusiliers' peacekeeping role during the Bosnian conflict in the last century.

There are countless hidden treasures too. These are the memories that the displays awaken for former fusiliers and their families and friends. Colin Lofthouse, who works at the museum and who himself served in the Fusiliers for 39 years, explained that once you became a fusilier, you were always a fusilier. The museum holds an important place in their hearts. 'It's like visiting family', added one visitor, who was a subaltern in the late 1980s and who was visiting with his daughter Katie.

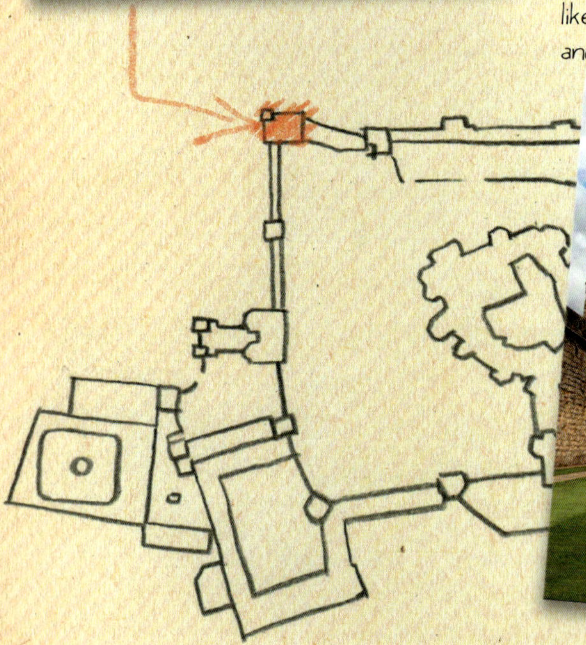

We asked Katie to explain what visiting the museum meant to her and this is what she wrote:

When I visited the museum, I was very surprised to see how much my family was involved:

Dad:- a proud officer of the R.N.F, who took some of the photos in Norway. These can be seen on the "Picture Wheel" game on the first floor.

Uncle:- an officer, who was involved in active service in Bosnia. He can be seen marching on one of the videos.

Great Great Grandad:- He was a soldier in the R.N.F in the First Word War, and died on the Somme.

Visiting the exciting memorial to all those brave men and women, hundreds of years ago and today, made me realise, there are some very special people in this world.

The museum meant so much to me and it shows that we are all touched in some way by history and if you look you will be too.

The Falconer's Tower

This tower is a 19th century replacement for the original 14th century falconer's tower.

What is a falconer?

Falcons were used for hunting. The falconer would train and care for the Percy family's birds. The falconer trained the hawk by carrying it around for hours on a glove. The bird was only fed while it was on the glove. In that way it came to associate feeding with being on the glove. The next part of training is to get the bird to fly short distances to the glove. It is tethered so that it can't fly away. When it lands on the glove, the falconer rewards it with food.

When the hawk has learned to return to the glove without hesitation, the hawk can fly free.

The falconer might use a dog to drive game towards the bird. The hawk would capture its prey. The falconer would need to be nearby to retrieve the hawk and give it a small food reward when it was back on the glove. If it was allowed to eat the prey, it would realise it could hunt its own food and would not return to the glove when it was flown.

The cross on the wall of the Falconer's Tower commemorates the Victoria Cross medal won by Lieutenant Colonel Henry Hugh Manvers Percy at the Battle of Inkerman (5 November 1854) during the Crimean War.

You can see his sword in the Guard Room of the keep.

The hawk's weight was carefully checked. It needed to be hungry before it would hunt.

Goshawks and sparrow hawks were used for hunting. Hawks were prized possessions and hawking was a sport of the nobility.

Records show some township rents paid to the second Lord Percy in 1335 were sixpence or a sparrow hawk.

The View from the Castle

When you are standing on the gun terrace, what you are standing on is a viewing platform. In 1760 the famous landscape gardener Lancelot 'Capability' Brown designed the panoramic view you are seeing. Brown gained his nickname 'Capability' from telling his wealthy clients that their parklands had 'great capability for improvement'. Capability thought nothing of having teams of workmen move a hill or alter the course of a river, or rebuild a bridge.

In the 19th century, in order that better views of the pastures and the Lion Bridge could be enjoyed in the Prudhoe Tower, some of the mediaeval castle walls were removed, the armourer's tower demolished and the Falconer's tower rebuilt.

The view from the bridge

The landscape was designed so that the first view of the castle is on the approach to the bridge. If you were a passenger in an old-fashioned horse drawn coach, the first view you would get would be when the coach crosses the bridge. The passengers' windows are on the sides of the coach. The bridge was rebuilt so that the passengers could marvel as the castle suddenly and dramatically appears, dominating the scene.

Cannons

English cannons were first used on the battlefield at the Battle of Crécy in 1346. The second Lord Percy's son and heir, Henry, was present at the battle and would have seen them in action, both there and at the siege of Calais in 1347. The cannons were not particularly effective in terms of firepower or accuracy. However, at Crécy, the cannon noise did terrify the horses of the French knights and caused them to veer away and collide with each other during a cavalry charge.

The newest are the two large cannons which were from the coastal defence battery at Alnmouth and were used by the Percy Artillery Volunteers until they were disbanded in 1906.

As the technology developed, cannons became increasingly important in warfare. Artillery fire could easily knock holes in castle walls. Castles were not secure from attackers in the way they had been. Military tactics changed.

The oldest are the four small 17th century bronze cannons, which were probably part of the castle defences.

The two bronze Portuguese cannons with the cast 'dolphin' handles were captured from the French army at the Battle of Vimiero in 1808 and brought to Alnwick Castle by Josceline Percy, then captain of HMS Hotspur.

The Postern Tower

The first Lord Percy built this tower. The postern gate or 'sally port' is one of only two exits to the mediaeval castle, the other being the main gateway and Barbican.

Strategically, the position of the tower was important. It could have provided flanking fire in the event of an attack on the keep.

Since 1836 it has housed a museum of relics collected by the Percy family and in particular those collected by the Fourth Duke, who was a passionate amateur archaeologist.

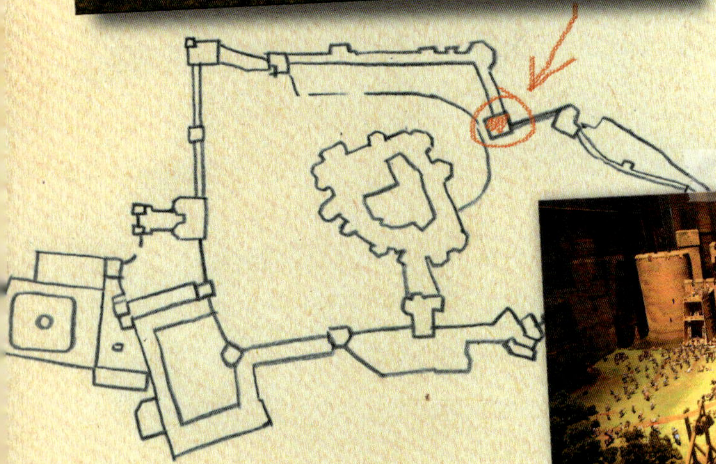

Why it was important to have a sally port?

Visit the exhibition about siege warfare at the base of the tower to find out!

Death and destiny

On the top floor is a display of the mysterious ancient 'cup and ring' stones. What do you think their meaning could be? Are they symbols of an ancient pagan religion? Do they represent the journey to an afterlife?

Digging history

The Percy family has a rich and colourful history and it is hardly surprising that different family members, over the generations, have been interested in history, whether as they were collectors, amateur archaeologists, sponsors of excavations (digs) or patrons of archaeologists.

There are some amazing objects in the collection, including a sword from the Battle of Otterburn, where Hotspur fought and the Shrewsbury shield, which was found on the field of battle where Hotspur was killed in 1403. Have a look at the shield. Do you think it could have been Hotspur's?

Also on display are some finds from Pompeii, the Roman town near Naples. Pompeii was covered in layers of ash from the volcanic eruption in 79 AD. The inhabitants of Pompeii were unprepared for this disaster. Those who fled once the volcano started erupting, stood a chance of survival. Those that took a chance on the eruption being short-lived did not survive.

The first Lord Percy built the Constable's Tower. It has not been altered or repaired, so it is as it was in the 14th century.

The Constable's Tower

The name of the tower is a mystery. No one really knows why it was called the Constable's Tower, because the constable would have had lodgings in the Middle Gatehouse. The constable would have been in charge of the castle if the family were away.

The Constable's Tower has an amazing and unique exhibition. The wooden training swords used by the Volunteers are extremely rare. Visit the tower to discover the fascinating story behind the Percy Tenantry Volunteers!

Could a 'Dad's Army' of local volunteers have taken on and held back Napoleon's army?

Napoleon's armies had been successful in Europe and his enemies had signed a peace treaty with him in October 1797. The only country left fighting Napoleon was Britain. Fears of French invasion led to preparations throughout the country. As Lord Lieutenant of Northumberland, the second Duke raised the Percy Yeomanry from his tenants.

Percy Tenantry Volunteers: Guerrilla fighters or Dad's Army?

Well trained and better supplied than the regular army, they were funded and commanded by the second Duke. The Duke had considerable military experience and was critical of how the British army was run. Having his own private army allowed him to try out his own ideas.

His experience of fighting in the American War of Independence led him to train his men as guerilla fighters. The American forces had used these tactics very effectively against the British.

The Percy Tenantry Volunteers had Riflemen's green coats (unlike the usual infantry red coats). They would have been difficult to spot in the green of the countryside. The uniforms were locally made.

Each man had a rifle that was far superior to the army issue Brown Bess musket. (A Brown Bess musket is on display in the Royal Northumberland Fusiliers Museum.) Ammunition was made at the castle, using gunpowder that the Duke bought directly from the manufacturers. Army ammunition frequently misfired, as crooked government agents would supply gunpowder bulked up with useless additives, so that they would make more profit.

The Percy Tenantry Volunteers had a plentiful supply of ammunition, both for training purposes and in case of invasion. This contrasted with ten rounds provided by the government for training and the further ten rounds for battle use.

There was a regiment of 1,500 volunteers, formed into three corps as riflemen, cavalry and artillery. The volunteers were well trained, well equipped and well disciplined. They were expected to do their duty or face the consequences. After all, being a volunteer had its advantages. A volunteer would escape the clutches of the Royal Navy's press gang. Life at sea was notoriously harsh.

The Percy Tenantry Volunteers never had to face invaders. Could they have held Napoleon's forces at bay until regular army reinforcements arrived? We will never know. What do you think?

There is a story about Rifleman Bell, who refused to carry one of the large wall guns. (You can see one of these guns on display in the coach house). Using the colourful language of the times, he said, 'I'll be damned if I carry anything heavier than a musket'.

This was reported to the Duke, who insisted that Rifleman Bell be sent to join the navy, where, he said, 'They damn those who'd rather be damned than do their duty.'

How fast could you load a musket?

1 Pull the hammer back till it clicks once (half cock)

2 Open the pan by pushing the frizzen open

3 "Bite the bullet" to open the cartridge, retain the ball in between the teeth, and put a pinch of powder in the pan

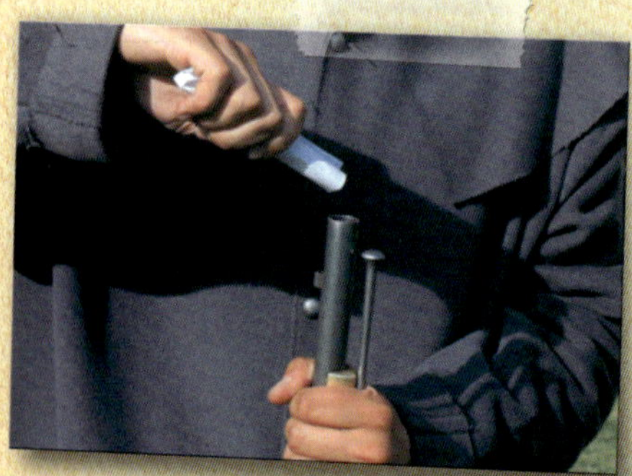

4 Close the pan, point the muzzle up by lowering the butt (grounding it in the case of a long arm) and pour the rest of the powder down the barrel.

5 Follow that with the ball – don't spit it down the barrel or it'll will be wet!

6 Use the ram rod to push the cartridge paper down as a wadding

Those weapons in the Lower Guard Chamber are most of the weapons used by the Cavalry arm of the PTV. There are about 240 swords and 190 pistols. Each of the 240 cavalrymen in the corps had one of each. The collection of the swords, the 1796 pattern light-cavalry sabre, is one of the best in private hands anywhere.

The pistols, as with the rifles used by the 1200 infantrymen, were loaded with a fairly strict procedure. Each man had a box of 20 or so cartridges and each of those contained a lead bullet and a measure of powder.

An expert's step-by-step quick-fire guide!

7 Remember to pull out the ram rod. If you fire with it still in the barrel, it will shoot out like an arrow – and how will you reload then?

8 Pull the hammer back till it clicks twice, full cock, trigger now active.

BANG!

9 Pull the trigger.
The hammer springs forward, and the flint in the hammer smashes into the frizzen, pushing it forward and spraying sparks of steel over the powder in the pan.
"Flash in the pan" is transmitted through the touch hole into the barrel and the main powder charge.

The weapon demonstrated here is a musket, but the procedure was the same for the Tenantry Volunteers' rifles.

The rifles' barrels had spiralling grooves cut into them, which span the bullets, making them more accurate over long distances.

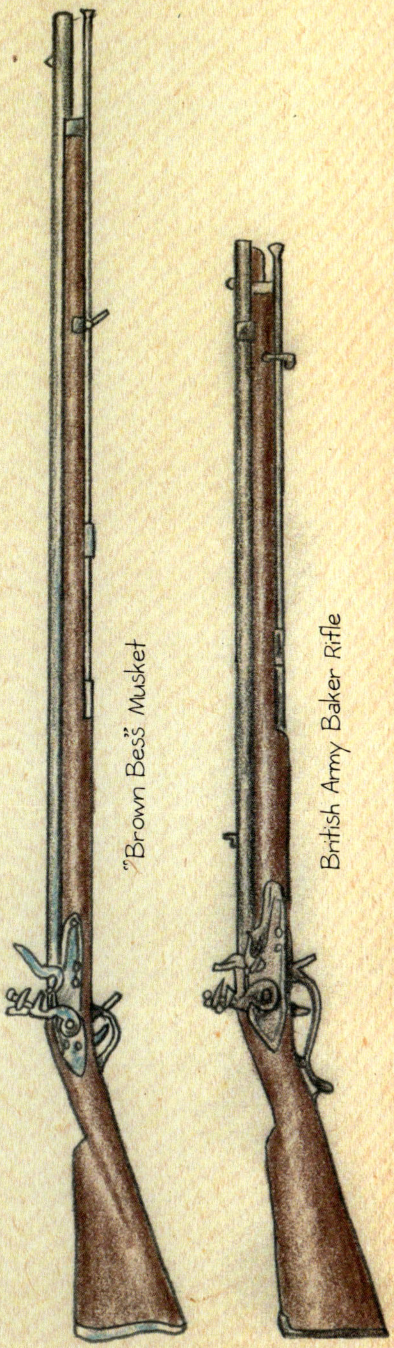

Brewers, Butchers and Bakers

Between the Postern tower and the Constable tower there used to be the bake house and the brew house.

Water was channelled to the brew house, where beer would have been made.

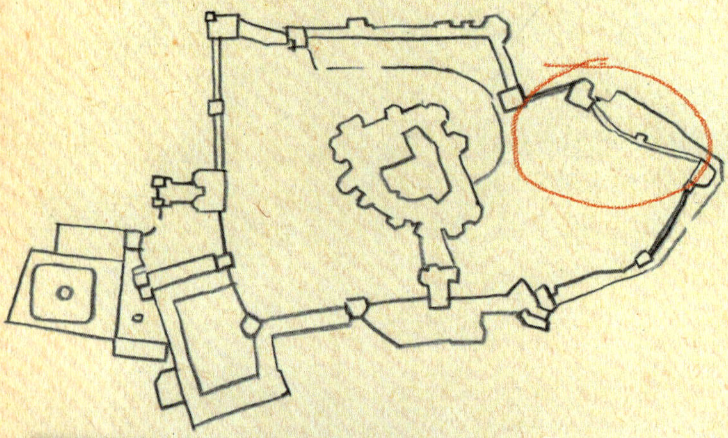

In mediaeval times beer was safer to drink than water, which might well be polluted. The alcohol killed off the bugs that made people sick.

Can you spot the blackening near the top of the wall where the chimneys once were?

The wall where the bake house ovens were looks reddish in colour. Can you see where the bake house was?

Some smaller buildings were attached to the bake house. These included a slaughterhouse, storeroom and a chantry house.

Payers for prayers

Priests would be paid to pray constantly for the lord's soul in the chantry house.

The Chapel

The chapel was an important feature of the castle. The mediaeval chapel would have been sited somewhere near the wall in front of Hotspur's seat. It would have been quite a large building. In 1512 there was a dean and ten priests serving the chapel. There were seventeen in the choir, including six choirboys. Mass was performed every morning at six.

However, in later centuries the family did not live in the castle and the chapel fell into ruins. In the 18th century, when the family returned to the castle, the first Duke had the ruins removed.

Hotspur's Seat

This part of the wall was originally built in the 14th century as a watchtower. The first Duke rebuilt it. The first Duchess, who was very proud of her ancestors, renamed it 'Hotspur's Seat'.

Exclusive! A Sneaky Peek inside the Record Tower!

The Record Tower is closed to the public. The Percy family records are stored there and have been on that site since the sixteenth century, although the tower itself has been rebuilt at different times.

Legal records are very important and most castles would have had a 'muniment' room. Muniment comes from a Latin word meaning 'defend' and legal documents were seen as a defence of the castle owner's rights and property. Christopher Hunwick, the current archivist who is in charge of the records, allowed us a sneaky peek inside the tower.

One of the most important documents is the original deed from 1309, when the castle was purchased. This would have been a vital piece of evidence if the dispute over castle ownership between Gilbert Atun and the second Lord Percy had ever been taken to court.

Lion Tower

The first Duke had added a gateway here so that he would have a second main entrance to the castle. In the nineteenth century the Fourth Duke removed two towers and built the Lion Tower.

Much filmed, the Lion Tower was the entrance to Hogwarts School and part of Nottingham Castle in Robin Hood Prince of Thieves.

Middle Gateway

The first Lord Percy built this as a single gatehouse that joined the keep with a curtain wall at the semi-circular tower.

There was a prison in the semi-circular tower in the middle gateway and a porter's lodge on the other side of the arch.

Over the centuries, various additions were made, including a nineteenth century tower.

Auditor's Tower/Beef Tower

The first lord of Alnwick built this tower in the fourteenth century. The auditor's tower may have gained its name from the imprisonment in it of one of the King's auditors, William Worme. The auditor would check the accounts and work out what tax would need to be paid. The sixth Earl wrote to Cardinal Wolsey, Henry VIII's chief minister, asking for a licence to imprison William Worme 'until he has accounted for more money received than ever I received.' Whether he was honest or not, Worme is a rather an unfortunate name for a taxman!

Other names for the tower are the Beef Tower and the Caterer's Tower because the tower used to house the castle's butchery.

Kitchen Tunnel

Near the keep, if you look on the ground, you will see some manhole covers with glass insets. These are in the service tunnel that runs from the kitchens to the dining room. The idea was that the kitchen staff could keep the food warm by bringing it though the tunnel.

In the Second World War, staff and pupils from Newcastle Church High School were evacuated to Alnwick and were staying in the castle. When the sirens went, everybody would go into the tunnel to shelter from the air raid.

West of the Beef Tower is the Clock Tower. A water tower used to stand on this spot.

The Final Defences

The second Lord Percy built the keep's two octagonal towers around 1340.

There would have been a drawbridge where the wooden walkway is now.

The dry moat would have been filled with sharp stakes and logs with sharp objects lashed to them. Attackers would have had to struggle through these before attacking the gateway.

The defenders of the keep

In mediaeval times the inner courtyard would have had a steep slope. This would allow archers to fire down at enemies coming through the archway. They would be able to shoot over the heads of the other defenders.

The well is 47 feet deep and 3 feet wide. It was supplied by spring water from a source outside the castle walls. Even if the rest of the castle's defences fell to the enemy, the defenders would still be able to hold out in the keep.

The stone statues

The statues on the keep and the middle gateway were put there in the fourteenth century. They had a military purpose as well as being for show. They were designed to put off archers aiming at castle defenders.

Coats of arms – family pride and a grim warning

The coats of arms were displayed as a matter of family pride. They also were there to let potential enemies know who the Percy allies were. If you took on the Percys, you could expect trouble from the families they had married into!

The archway

Eustace Fitz John (de Vesci) built the archway in the middle twelfth century. It has a chevron (dog's tooth) pattern design. If you look carefully you can see the difference between the original stone work of the original keep, which was constructed hurriedly and the later work by the second Lord Percy. The first keep had to be put up in a hurry, to provide protection for the Norman family who lived in it.

Dreadful dungeons

As you enter the keep, if you go into the doorway on the right, you can see an oubliette or 'bottle' dungeon. 'Oubliette' comes from a French word that means 'forget'. Prisoners would be forgotten. They might have food and water lowered down to them, but otherwise the guards weren't too worried about keeping an eye on them. For a prisoner thrown into the oubliette, there was no chance of escape. The dungeon was in the shape of a bottle. The only opening is the small top of the 'bottle' (two feet square). The dungeon is eleven feet deep and has a floor area of nine feet by eight feet.

There was also a second dungeon and guardroom on the other side of the gateway.

In the border ballad, The Fair Flower of Northumberland, a Scottish prisoner escapes with the help of, and accompanied by, the Fair Flower of Northumberland (in one version, the earl's daughter), on expensive horses belonging to her father. This was something which prisoners might have dreamed about. Dreams were their only escape from the grim reality of the dreadful dungeons.

Raising the roof

Maintaining a castle in good repair is a huge undertaking. The castle roof renovation and repairs started in September 2005. These photographs were taken in 2007 and show the roofers working on the keep. Because the castle is an important historical building, the roof has to be renovated in the same way as it was originally constructed.

The castle roofs are made of lead. The original 18th century roofing has been taken down and the lead recycled using a traditional process. Once melted down, the lead is cast on a bed of sand, then drawn out and milled. The new rolls of lead roofing are hoisted up the same way as they always have been, as the previous roofers would have used ropes and pulleys too. Now, of course, the hoists are electrically powered.

Making their mark!

If you look closely at the original mediaeval walls of the castle you will see the mason's marks. In the entrance passageway to the Postern Tower alone, fourteen different marks have been spotted. These marks identified what section of wall each mason had built. The marks were used to work out how much each mason should be paid. We can tell from the marks that some of the same masons worked on other castles. For example, similar marks to the ones in the Constable's Tower have been found at Dunstanburgh Castle. The building work at Dunstanburgh Castle began in 1313, around the same time that the first lord was having work done here at Alnwick Castle. Have you spotted a mason's mark?

The Keep's Surprise Inside!

Take a moment to look at the lantern and the doorknocker. They are clues as to what you will find inside the keep. If you are expecting a mediaeval-style interior inside the mediaeval castle, you are in for a surprise!

The doorknocker was made in Venice in the 17th century and the lantern is copy of one from an Italian palace (the Palazzo Echo in Florence). There is an Italian theme coming through here – be prepared for luxurious marble floors and walls, amazing decorated ceilings and splendid statues!

The 4th Duke loved 16h century art and design. He decided to follow the Italian fashion by keeping the outside of the mediaeval castle as it was, while filling the interior with wonderful works of art.

Powder horns and pistols

The arms and equipment on display are those used by the Percy Tenantry Volunteers and date from 1798–1815. The powder horns would have held gunpowder ready for loading the firearms. On display are 212 pistols and 418 powder horns. There are also 32 carbine bayonets, 116 leather powder pouches, 9 halberds (a halberd is a sort of axe on a pole), 8 bugles and 15 sergeants' swords. There are also a lot of cavalry sabres (these were swords soldiers on horseback would use). Have a guess – how many you think there might be?

Alnwick Castle and the Civil War

The suits of armour on display in the Lower Guard Room were left at the castle by Cromwell's forces.

How 3,000 Scottish prisoners of war 'disappeared'!

In 1650, Cromwell's army captured 6,000 Scottish prisoners at the Battle of Dunbar. The prisoners were taken to Durham. A letter to the Earl's auditor, written at the time, states that the prisoners spent one night at the castle.

According to one historian, Bates, whose History of Northumberland was published in 1895, the prisoners spent eight days at the castle and 3,000 Scots died of starvation and exposure. True enough, the weather was reported to have been terrible and it may be that prisoners may have died from the cold and wet on the way down to Alnwick.

However, any dead would have been given Christian burials and there are no records of a mass grave.

The same historian, Bates, claimed that many more prisoners died at Morpeth on the way to Durham. The half-starved men were given rotten cabbages to feast on. As a result, he claims, many died.

The truth

Hmm, who is telling the truth here? How did this story come about? Could it have anything to do with the fact that the people of Alnwick were loyal to the king and hated Cromwell and his 'Roundhead' supporters? Cromwell had already gained a reputation for brutality in Ireland. This tragic tale certainly adds to it!

What do you think happened to the 3,000 men? Did they die, or were they allowed to return home quietly? Which makes the more exciting story?

Royalist or Roundhead?

Algernon, the tenth Earl of Northumberland, started out by supporting Parliament, but strongly opposed the trial and execution of the king. His views were respected by both sides.

The Ballad of Chevy Chase

Where's Harry?

Harry Hotspur was born above the gatehouse in the keep. You were never likely to get very far into the Alnwick home of the Duke of Northumberland without some reference to the great warrior!

Where's Harry? Look up in the Upper Guard Chamber to see the 'Chevy Chase' paintings. The four panels form a frieze around the top of the walls. They are a series of oil paintings by Francis Götzenburg, and were painted between 1863–1864.

The Ballad of Chevy Chase, also known as The Hunting of the Cheviot, survived in two versions. Both were collected in Thomas Percy's The Reliques of Ancient English Poetry. The story has historical characters in it, but basically it is all made up. Percy, from the references to the Battle of Otterburn, is Hotspur. The ballad would have been sung and was extremely popular in its day.

The story of Chevy Chase

Percy and his followers go deer hunting on Douglas's land. Douglas swears he will put a stop to the hunt.

He and his followers find Percy and his men and challenge them to say what men they were and who had given them permission to hunt there. Fairly pointless, since Douglas knew the answers to both questions. Percy's men refuse to say who they are. Douglas calls Percy by name and challenges him to single combat. One of Percy's men refuses to stand by while Percy and Douglas fight.

Fighting breaks out and everyone joins in. Percy and Douglas are fighting when an arrow fatally wounds Douglas. As Percy sees Douglas dying (this is the tear-jerking bit), he realises what a brave man and skilled fighter Douglas was. He says, 'Wo ys me for the' (Woe is me for you). Too late, he wishes he could have saved Douglas's life. Before Percy has an opportunity to say any more, one of Douglas' followers, Sir Hugh Montgomery, runs him through with a spear. The two sides continue to fight until very few are left alive.

After the battle, weeping widows came to collect the bodies of their men. The dead men were carried away on biers made of tree branches. Both the kings of Scotland and England mourn the deaths of Douglas and Percy. King Harry (Henry) gets his revenge at the 'battel of Humbyll-down' (Battle of Humbleton Hill).

The old version has a powerful opening and gets straight to the point:

The Persè owt of Northombarlonde
    And a vowe to God mayd he
That he wolde hunte in the mountayns
    Off Chyviat within dayes thre,
In mauger of doughtè Dogles
    And all that ever with him be.

The Percy from Northumberland
Swore an oath to God
That he would hunt in the mountains
Of Cheviot within three days
In spite of fierce Douglas
And all that ever were with him.

The Library of the Fourth Duke

Algernon, 4th Duke of Northumberland, became Duke at the age of 55 in 1847, after the death of his brother Hugh. He had served in the Royal Navy during the Napoleonic War, starting as a midshipman at thirteen and captaining a warship at the age of twenty-three.

When the war ended, Algernon left the navy. His seafaring past had a strong influence on him. Algernon was a great supporter and patron of the lifeboat movement, providing some of the stations along the Northumberland coast with boats at his own expense. He built the Sailors' Home at North Shields to provide for the welfare of seaman on land.

The 4th Duke equipped the library with a weather station.

The weather station has a clock, barometer and wind indicator. Daily weather records were kept and provided useful information for predicting the weather.

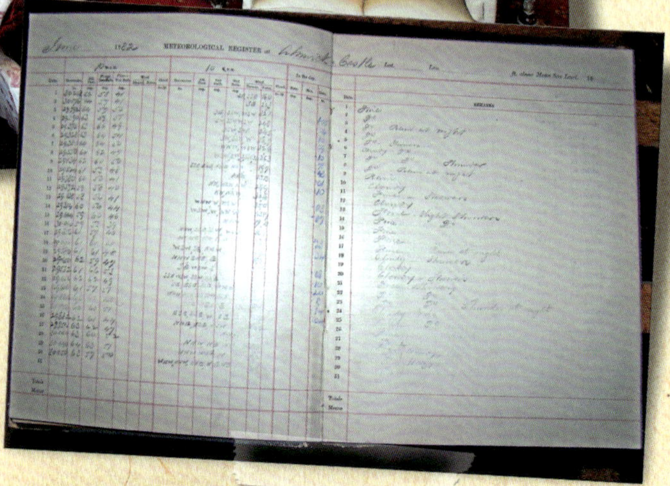
METEOROLOGICAL REGISTER

The ceiling

The ceiling was designed by Montirolli to reflect the 4th Duke's great interests.

We know about Duke Algernon's passion for Italian art from the interior design of the castle.

One of his other interests was astronomy. Algernon had supported the work of astronomer Sir John Hershel. He accompanied Hershel to study the southern constellations at Cape Colony and had paid for the publication of Herschel's work. As a result, Algernon was made a fellow of the Royal Society and of the Astronomical Society.

Archaeology was another of his passions, particularly the study of ancient Egypt.

Look at the ceiling. What do you think represents Duke Algernon's passion for archaeology? What might show his enthusiasm for astronomy?

The books

There are thousands of them, dating from 1475 until around 1910. Guess how many there are!

A squirrel's tale

This bushy-tailed bookworm is one of several stuffed animals at Alnwick Castle. Preserving creatures in this way is called taxidermy. This was very popular in Victorian times. Often pets and others that were well-liked found special places around the home. In fact, as you can see, this well "read" squirrel has found a good spot in the library.

Answer: There are 14,500 books.

Fabulous China

The china on display in the China Gallery is very rare and very precious. The Meissen factory in Germany made the oldest and most valuable pieces.

What is Meissen China and what is special about it?

In the seventeenth century porcelain was known as 'white gold' and it was very, very expensive. It was imported from Japan and China.

In Europe, two alchemists working for Augustus the Strong, ruler of Saxony, discovered how to make true hard paste porcelain. The alchemists were attempting to make gold, which is what alchemists used to try to do. Instead, they stumbled upon the recipe for porcelain, which in those days was as precious as gold. As Augustus was a passionate collector of porcelain, their discovery was especially welcome. The discovery was made in 1710. Production of porcelain started in the town of Meissen soon after.

Top secret

The porcelain recipe was kept secret. Very few workers knew how the porcelain was made. Those who did might only know part of the process.

Diplomatic gift and lottery prize

Augustus, and his son Augustus III, used the porcelain when doing deals with foreign governments. The highly prized china was the sort of gift that was given when treaties were signed or favours given.

The older Meissen china service was a gift to British diplomat, Sir Charles Hanbury-Williams in April 1747. It arrived in London in 1751 and was displayed at Holland House. We don't know how the Duke of Northumberland came to own it, other than a note stating he had won it in a lottery.

Birds and hunting

If you love wild birds then you'll think the soup plates are super! Meissen artists copied them from books of engravings by an English naturalist, Eleazar Albin. On the other pieces of the service there is a hunting theme. Many of the animals shown are ones that would have been hunted. There are some very strange illustrations too. Look out for weird rhinos, some sinister mermaids and an odd-looking elephant!

Aesop's Fables

The other Meissen sevice features scenes from Aesop's fables. Jean-Baptiste Oudry had illustrated French author Jean De La Fontaine's translation of Aesop's Fables. The Meissen artists copied the pictures for their plate designs. You have probably heard the fable about the race between the tortoise and the hare. Can you find the plate?

Flawless china?

When the porcelain was made there were sometimes tiny flaws or faults. The artists decorating the china came up with an ingenious way of covering them up. Have a look and see if you can guess what it was!

If you guessed right then, there are no flies on you! You may see lots of them on the china!

The Dining Room

Dining in aristocratic style

The Dining Room is in the same area of the castle as the original mediaeval banqueting hall. The Percy family has been eating here and entertaining their guests for generations.

How many can sit down for a meal? The magnificent Victorian mahogany table extends to seat forty people.

The silver gilt candelabra, dishes and plates were made between 1822–1830, by London silversmiths Rundell, Bridge and Rundell. This dining service was taken to France and used when the 3rd Duke was the King's representative at the coronation of Charles X. (The Duke's efforts were very much appreciated. By a unanimous vote of both Houses of Parliament, he was presented with the ceremonial sword that is displayed in this room.)

Norman Tulip's walking sticks

The display of walking sticks is unique. These 35 sticks are the work of the celebrated craftsman, Norman Tulip, who used to live nearby at Denwick. The sticks took from 70 hours (for a fairly simple design) to 400 hours to make.

The handles are made from rams' horns. These are heated and shaped over a spirit burner. One of the walking stick handles was made from a horn of one of the rare Chillingham cattle (the stick on the second left in the photograph). The shanks of the walking sticks were made from a variety of woods, including hazel, blackthorn, plum and holly. Five-inch pins fixed the handles to the shanks.

The stick Norman thought was perfect is the plain one. The unblemished horn handle is what made it special.

The decoration of the handles was painstaking work. Norman used inks to colour the horns. The spots on the trout were put on using the chewed end of a matchstick.

Norman Tulip, who died in 1995, was an Honorary Freeman of the Horners' Company. He was very proud of the fact that one of his sticks was presented to Prince Charles, who is the Patron of the Border Stick Dressers' Association.

Pride of place: portraits of 1st Duke and Duchess

The magnificent portraits of the first Duke and Duchess, painted by Sir Joshua Reynolds, are rightly given pride of place above the fireplace in the dining room. Without the first Duchess' pride in this place, Alnwick Castle, it might well have become a ruin. Without her pride in her ancestry, the family name Percy would not have continued. The Duchess had persuaded her husband, then Sir Hugh Smithson, to adopt the family name Percy.

The Drawing Room

Next to the dining room is the drawing room, where family and guests would "withdraw" to after their meal, to enjoy a conversation, or a friendly game of cards.

One feature of the drawing room is this spinning wheel, which was used to turn wool into yarn. Can you see how it worked?

The Five Senses Table - A Feast for the Eyes!

Imagine someone asked you to design a table, with illustrations depicting the five senses. What ideas would you have for touch, hearing, smell, taste and sight?

You can compare your ideas with the amazing Five Senses table in the drawing room.

Charles P. Slocombe designed the table for the 4th Duke, who died before it was completed.

The library table was made from walnut. The designs are made from intricately inlaid wood vemeers. Veneers are thin layers of wood, carefully glued together. A fine saw is used to cut the fragile vemeers. Marquetry, as this technique is called, is a time-consuming process. It took years to craft this table. Blakes of London began work in 1854 and the table was finished in 1865.

The craftsmen who worked on this table used many different types of wood, as well as mother of pearl for the serpent's eyes and ivory for its teeth. The blue wood was stained holly.

What makes crystal chandeliers sparkle so brightly?

There are two reasons. Firstly, the glass is cut so that each glass drop catches the light, like jewels do. The light is reflected in the glass. Not only that, when the light passes from air through the glass, the rays of light change direction.

Secondly, the crystal is made differently from ordinary glass. A chemical called lead oxide is added when the glass is molten (very hot and melted). The type of glass that results from this mix is called lead crystal. This has more sparkle because light travels through it more slowly than normal glass. Crystal with a high lead content has the most sparkle.

Revealed at last! The dark secret of a famous artist!

As you explore the State Rooms, you will discover a number of paintings by famous Italian artist Canaletto. Canaletto was born in Venice in 1697. His real name was Giovanni Antonio Canal. His father, Benardo Canal, was also a painter and this is why his son got the nickname 'Canaletto', Canal junior. Canal is a very appropriate name for a Venetian artist, as the city is famous for its canals!

As you look at Canaletto's landscapes, you will notice that they have an almost photographic accuracy. Yet the pictures were painted long before the invention of photography. How did Canaletto achieve this effect?

One of the paintings by Canaletto on display in the castle is this one of Northumberland House in London. This was the London home of the Duke of Northumberland at the time, and overlooked Trafalgar Square until 1874, when it was demolished after a fire.

Canaletto had come to England because most of the customers for his paintings were English, and war in Europe made it difficult for them to come to Venice.

The Duke of Northumberland was one of the many wealthy Englismen of the time who hired Canaletto to paint views of their homes.

It's all done by mirrors!

The secret was a device known as a camera obscura. This is a lens attached to a box (or even a tent). The inside of the box is dark. The box would be positioned in front of the view that was to be painted. Light from the landscape passed through the lens and a smaller upside down image of the landscape was projected onto a surface inside the box. Using an angled mirror, the right way up image can be projected and the image traced. Canaletto would use these tracings when sketching his preparatory drawings.

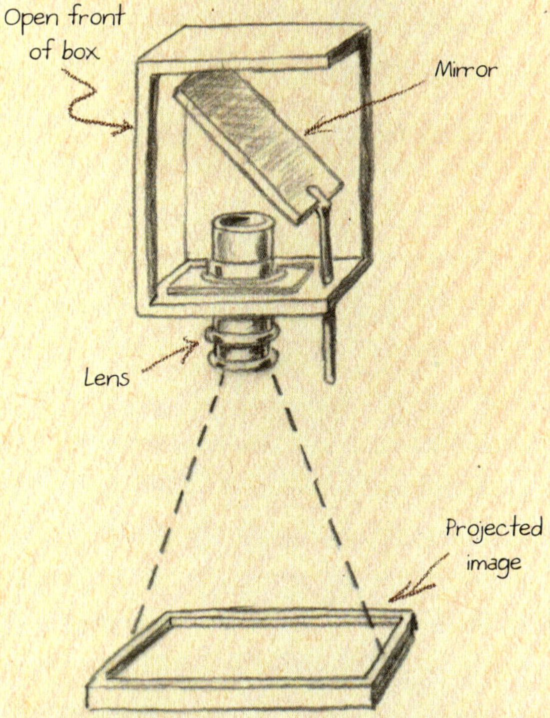

Be an art critic!

The camera obscura explains Canaletto's technique. His genius is what he brought to that technique. What makes him a great artist? Is it the use of light, colour and the atmosphere of his landscapes? Is it the skill with which he selects and organises the view (the composition of the picture)? Have a good look at these great works of art. What do you think makes them special?

Exclusive!

Castle Cat Reveals All!

Bunyip, the official pet in residence at Alnwick Castle, tells us about his early upbringing in the stables. 'Those were the days,' he sighs. 'The horses used to be where the Knights' Quest area is now. I lived there with my brother and we spent many happy hours catching mice. An Australian girl who was working as a stable hand gave me my name. It is an Australian word that means 'devil' or 'spirit'. I prefer spirit, myself.'

Bunyip's brother sadly died in a road traffic accident on the Lion Bridge. 'You can't be too careful when crossing the road!' Bunyip advises.

As castle cat, Bunyip has his own human, Mandy, who provides him with meals. 'Mandy is very good to me. I can overlook the worm tablets. I suppose she means well. In the summer, she treats me to tubs of ice cream on very hot days.'

It isn't all catnaps and ice cream though, being Alnwick Castle's cat. 'Sometimes I feel I am the most stroked cat in the country,' says Bunyip. 'The young visitors all feel they have to give me a pat. Sometimes it gets too much and I feel I need a bit of space. Then, just when I have found a nice quiet spot for a sleep, I hear a voice and I just dread what is coming... 'Is it stuffed?' The next thing I know I am being prodded – 'No it's not!' Then it's more patting. You need the patience of a saint in this job.'

At night Bunyip often tours the castle and on cold nights he will keep company with the security guards.

We asked Bunyip if he has ever seen a ghost in the castle. 'One night we did see a ghastly figure wandering around the keep and heard blood-curdling yelling – the same name, over and over,' he says. 'It was one of the family calling after one of the dogs that had got out!'

Bunyip does not think the Castle is haunted. 'There is only one spirit in this castle', he says firmly, 'and that is me!'